AF610564

# Ask Satan

 To contact the author email: mjefte2000@yahoo.com

ISBN 978-1-257-01134-6

ACKNOWLEDGEMENTS

Though this book is dedicated only to ME, it is worth mentioning the help of:

G.A Chaves

Sonia Fernandez

Natalia Rossi

## Foreword

Ask Satan (the book) is a collection of Michelle J. Wong's columns from his homonymous online project (he is twitching now as you read the word "homonymous").

Michelle J. Wong turns the table at that empty Christian rhetoric, "What Would Jesus Do?" He answers it with a "What Would Satan Say?," and delivers a more clear-eyed, worldly approach to his subjects in these mock-motivational columns. He addresses topics ranging from politics to relationships, from theology to diets, war, sex and self-esteem; and triggers laughter, roars and blasphemy.

The book is organized in five sections dealing each with a specific topic: Family, Dating & Relationships, Society, Politics, Religion & Existentialism.

The questions remained unedited—they were taken as-is from emails sent to Satan. Anything heavenly or christian is not capitalized. ie...heaven, jesus, god.

# Dating & Relationships

***Dear Lord of the Reeking Hole,***

***I wanted to ask you, what is the most ergonomic sex position? And is it true that Muslims get a bunch of virgins when they die?***

***What do atheists get?***

***Love,***

***Pleasure Hunter***

Dear Pleasure Hunter,

Oh, boy!

Don't you just love how mortals come out of a pussy just to spend the rest of their lives trying to get right back into one?

For a sentimental dreamer and hopeless romantic like you, the most ergonomic sex position would probably be the one in which you are sitting in front of your computer while watching a web cam whore undress herself.

However, any position that keeps you from injuring yourself while you are trying to dick-slap someone in the face, as well as any position that keeps you from getting squirted in the face can be defined as ergonomic.

These positions can vary from partner to partner, depending on your sizes, her sizes, your looks, her looks and your level of drunkenness.

Here is some advice:

1. **Lift with your legs, not with your back**. While maneuvering your partner to the appropriate height for hiding the salami, take a moment to assess whether you can actually lift her *at all*. If she is not a super fat meatloaf and you actually can, make sure you keep your back straight and use your legs to leverage her.

This may be difficult if you're into what is euphemistically called big, beautiful women, or BBW (scientifically known as *Big Booty Bitch With A Ham's Face* or BBBWAHF, for short).

In this case you might need the assistance of a dolly or a forklift so you can put the bitch up for inspection.

Good luck finding the clit in those layers of lumpy lumps surrounding her tunnel.

If you can't get any extra muscle or hydraulic power, you may have to settle for rolling her into position—though that might take 365 days if you are planning to roll the fat bitch all the way around.

Make sure you take some flares in case you get lost exploring that cave and don't forget a flash light and a machete for the pubes.

2. **Do not twist.** In. Out. In. Out. This is not a dance routine; you don't get points for contorting.

Your partner, however, does. Leave the twisting around to her, especially if she's ugly. Ask her to twist her face away from you.

3. **Maintain your center of balance.** Not as easy as you think, especially if you have had a few gallons of beer, though if the bitch is a BBBWAHF, don't worry because they tend to have their own gravitational center.

Now, if you can't stand up to save your life, lower *your* center of balance. Kneel, or lie down and make her do all the work. Fuck it: let women do all the work regardless!

Here is why:

I once saw this chick with whom I wanted to try all the positions I could, ergonomic or not.

She was so hot that I just wanted to rip her clothes off and scream at her pussy in anger for no reason at all.

I would have fucked her in the pooper so hard that silent farts would have just fallen out of her ass every time she tried to walk away from me.

Yeah you heard me; I wanted to hit that ass till she started speaking in tongues.

**I wanted to eat fried chicken off her big ol' ass so bad that I even asked her out on a date to KFC.**

Anyway, I forgot where I was going with this... So from now on I'm just going to leave the rest of this book blank.[1]

Still, your question is retarded and so is your face. And, as far as atheists and Muslims go, when they die, they all come to Hell just like you will.

Burn!

–Satan

P.S. In Hell atheists will be the Muslims' virgins, so keep doubting a higher existence.

1 Umm… no. Actually, you are not. (Publisher's Note).

***D** ear Satan,*

*I was wondering, what does the Prince of Darkness like to eat? I would like to have a date with you.*

*I'm a professional chef and I was cooking for jesus the other day, but all he likes to eat is fish. He'll eat bread and drink wine too, but he keeps telling me it's his body and his blood. Which is kinda gross if you ask me…*

*So, what do you like to eat? Maybe I can come and cook for you some time.*

*Iron Chef*

Dear Iron Chef,

I am a voracious glutton. And deciding what to eat in this truly treacherous food landscape that life has become is not an easy task.

However, in much the same way as emotionally unstable women are fantastic in bed, unhealthy food is unbelievable in my mouth—I love to eat unhealthy food and drink girls pretty.

So, if you cook only healthy shit and try to cook it for me, I will rearrange your face.

**I am on a strict diet of alcohol and Tabasco**. But I do love mayonnaise wrapped in bacon.

*Nothing* comes close to greasy food. Salad gives me diarrhea and tofu isn't really food. The only thing better than mayonnaise wrapped in bacon is bacon wrapped in mayonnaise with Tabasco on it. I once went to IHOP because that's all they serve there, and **I was so excited I was howling like a dog with his dick stuck in a vacuum.**

Suddenly, this salad eating hag who I'm pretty sure had tentacles coming out of her vagina asked me to keep it down.

So I asked my waitress to pass her a note that said:

*Dear lady, please check one of the following:*

***How would you like me to ruin your dinner?***

*a. Cooking you alive*

*b. Serving your meal at an inappropriate temperature*

*c. Through a communicable disease*

What was funny about this particular situation is that this obese bitch thought she looked really sexy having salad at her engagement dinner party.

I was like, "You're fat and your gay husband is going to cheat on you." And then the husband was like, "She is the sexiest girl in the world," because he was under the influence of voodoo or beer goggles or something.

Then I was like, "Yeah, if you stretch the concept of sexy as far as her stretch marks, then she is sexy indeed."

Then right before I shoved my foot up his ass he said, "C'mon man we don't want any trouble!"... So as you can see, eating healthy will only get your ass kicked.

Why stress about pesticides, insecticides, fertilizers, poison, birth defects, tofurky, sanitation standards, irritable bowel syndrome and intestines? **That hippie shit is for Hare Krishnas and Rastafarians.**

Now, I see you've been cooking for *jesus.* How'd that go?

Did he try to multiply the fish? That explains why his breath always smells like a vagina. He is a jerk like that—I don't know why the whole resurrection thing made him feel so special.

**Dracula did it too and so did the zombies!**

Anyway, if you want to cook for me, think about a Southern menu, get creative, maybe some panda meat? And remember the fun part: *Gluttony is a sin.*

Cheers,
–Satanlicious

**D** ***ear Dark Lord,***

***I am not sure how to say this…***

***First, let me tell you a little bit about myself.***

***I am a very hot, flexible dancer that enjoys reading your blog.***

***I find you captivating, honestly. And well, I would like to have sex with you.***

***Not only raw pulsing wild sex, but a sensual real connection with you as well.***

***I think we could be perfect for each other.***

***Do me.***

***Best,***

***Sexy Satan lover***

Dear Sexy Satan lover,

Among the millions of things you forgot to mention about my greatness, such as the well known fact that I have American bald eagles that fly around my head because of my eminence and penile fortitude, you failed to include how testicularly hallowed I am—one of the many reasons why you want my balls of fire so *badly*.

**Contrary to what many think, *I*, not god, invented sex.**

Specifically with: animals, children, old people and mental patients.

Therefore, wanting me is perfectly normal, and almost vital.

Once you see the sun, you want the summer. I get it—it's all about looking right and feeling wrong after.

However, my offending beef-dong is worth only the best women's bearded birth canals in the universe and some ugly hag like you in your mid- or late thirties does not deserve a piece of this banana pie.

Die,
–SATAN

P.S. Help me win the war against nature and cut a tree or two while you wait for my call.

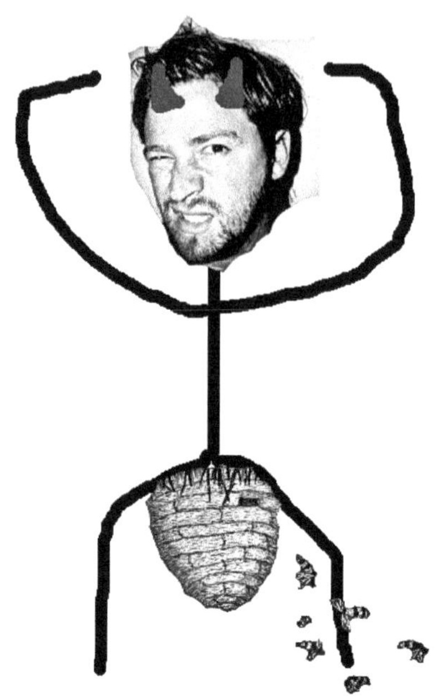

***D** ear Satan,*

***Recently I had sex with a dirty prostitute in Tijuana and that bitch gave me ghanneria.***

***I was wondering if I should tell my girlfriend or just spread the wealth and blame it on her.***

***Eli kamisher***

Dear Eli kamisher,

Yes, the presence of disease or infirmity has always been a concern to all of us.

You probably have nothing to worry about since "ghanneria" is not even a fucking word (as opposed to "illiterate") and therefore probably *not* a disease.

To a Don Juan like you, ghanneria probably sounds like a distant relative of Gonorrhea.

However, **you might want to learn how to spell before you go to TJ and put Tapatío sauce on your dick while stuffing a dirty pink taco**.

You might need to read the instructions of your antibiotics later, and god and your 3rd grade teacher know that's not easy for you.

That reminds me of the time when sweet baby jesus was actually just a little kid, and god was trying to teach him how to walk on water.

However, sweet baby jesus kept fucking up and turning the water into wine.

At this, god, tired and drunk, told sweet baby jesus, "I shall spank thy sweet baby arse till I get sober," he then punched him... and pitied him *three times* before he hit the ground.

The moral of the story is: you were lucky Miss Marshall was your 3rd grade teacher and not god.

Anyway, getting back to your infested genitals:

Casually exchanging pesos for sexual encounters will probably contract you some real live hazardous STD that will make your dick smell like a crusty cauliflower and look like a beehive in two weeks.

However, if this happens, don't get caught up in the details of who infected who, or which medications are appropriate for your disease. Such musings are beside the point.

You should simply blame your girlfriend as your reputation might be damaged by the moral depravities of sleeping with a lovely TJ hooker.

As far as spreading the wealth, *go for it*.

You see, once everyone in your community knows you have STDs you will become the town's leper. And this will turn you into a minority—like black people in college or like Mexicans who don't live under a wheelbarrow with all their cousins.

Nevertheless, **chub-rubbing the love before everyone realizes you are the plague purveyor is crucial**. That way a fair sense of equality will be created in your elitist community and no one can say, "Eli, your balls look like a beehive." Since *everyone's* would.

I know, thank me later.

Rot,

–SATAN

P.S. In Hell, STD stands for "see the doctor."

***D** ear Satan,*

***Who among us meer mortals is worthy enough to date the King of Darkness?***

***I dated a goth vamp but never anyone demonic!***

***Where would Satan go on a date?***

***Somewhere hot I suppose!***

***Alexa Jones***

Dear Alexa Jones,

It is *futile* to pretend that anyone deserves my dark-namic company, *for I Am Supreme*.

However, if you ever got offered to join me on a date—which most likely will consist of me sodomizing virgins while you watch—you don't question this decision twice, *you raise the roof.*

You heard me, bitch? Raise the fucking roof, because we are not going to be playing water polo where I am taking you.

On the other hand, after dating a big-shot Goth Vamp you should not hold your breath waiting for me to call you.

Now, to answer your question regarding me, and dating; this is what I usually do on dates:

I like to drive my date around and let her experience a fair amount of what road rage really means.

This is well known for making girls horny.

This one time, I was recklessly driving my rape-date to show her this awesome basement I had told her about.

Suddenly, some blind senior citizen got in my way and I was forced to give him a ride back to the old-people-home.

When I got there I asked the janitor to get a plastic bag and a shovel so I could drop him off, and this chick got so horny she said to me, **"My ass is a playground and it is recess."**

What can I say? I like to cut loose sometimes.

I realize that in this society, transmitting an undesirable sexual disease or stabbing someone on a first date is looked down upon, but that's what Craigslist was for.

Have a nice day,

–SATAN

***D** ear Satan,*

***I probably should have asked this when it was relevant during my life.***

***However, I figured it doesn't hurt to plan for the future. I am trying to be more proactive about things.***

***Anyway, I was wondering, have you ever had your heart broken? If so, what did you do to make the whole process go by faster?***

***If not, what would you recommend for us humans? Oh and one last thing, what advice would you give to become a better heartbreaker? Sometimes I like to make others feel bad***

***Yours truly,***

***Proactive***

Dear Proactive,

A broken heart is the bittersweet reek of the living.

Despite the fact that I can't get my heart broken—because I don't have one, or a liver—I happen to know everything there is to know about this topic.

**First, I cannot sigh hard enough to show my frustration with you.**

Second, I would like to point out that you probably have been a little more *poonactive*[2] than proactive. This is what keeps getting your heart broken.

I mean, jesus! When will you learn your lesson and stop letting people shove their fist up any available orifice of your body while jumping from relationship to relationship?

2 The state in which a woman's thoughts and actions are controlled solely by her pussy (Dr. Satan's Note)

Oh, and when I say “jesus!” I meant it more like an exclamation not like the noun—I don’t really like that guy.

Anyway, you have to protect relationships such as marriage from breaking up so that this doesn’t happen often to you.

However, if your heart has already been broken, there is only **one thing you can do to speed up your internal recovery: Replacement.**

This one time some stupid girlfriend I had named Katrina—I know, it sounds like the name of a medicine that someone from Star Trek wouldn’t even take—decided to dump me.

I know what you are thinking: “But Satan, how dare she even consider leaving you?

She should be rolling over and *taking it in the corn hole* at your command”—which is true.

Nevertheless, I didn’t care because of my toughness and manly lack of heart. And of course because every time someone pronounced her name I would reply, “Gesundheit!”

On the other hand, she was brokenhearted. She would cry and tell all her friends about how jealous she would get every time I cheated on her… how I was having orgies with so many chicks that my kids were being born beige and how that affected our intimacy and such nonsense.

After the misery of being away from me, she tried to get back together. But what happened?

I had already replaced her ass for a Mini Cooper-driving hipster girl who didn't mind drinking pure alcohol and who rocked at *Guitar Hero*. BAM!

As you can see, replacing was the quickest way to forget about Katrina's existence. She now sucks cock for cigarettes.

Now, to answer your question on how to break a heart, here are some tips that I feel could be useful when breaking up with a partner, despite how long you have been together:

1. **Minimize the meaning this relationship had in your life.** Burn all gifts, cards, pictures or anything stupid that reminds you of your partner, even if this involves pets, family members, or even your partner. Once these items catch their porches on fire, run; then repeat. But this time leave a note that says—never mind don't leave a note… that's evidence.

2. **While breaking up, don't forget to restate your differences** such as, "Look, you like opera, I like *Ren & Stimpy*, you like being fat and ugly, I don't like fat ugly people," and such.

3. **Don't forget the classic, "It's not you, it's me."** *I* am the one who has been cheating on you with random chicks; it's not you, it's *me*!

4. **At the end of your conversation say, "You will be OK, you are a big man (or girl),"** then point at their fattest body part, and laugh at the irony of semantics.

5. **Come back later and ask if you left any condoms at his/her house**, and explain you might need those back.

If you are breaking up with someone because this person is ugly, remember beauty is in the eye of the beer holder.

Therefore, there are no ugly people, only sober beer holders.

Cheers,

–SATAN

P.S. You will never find anyone who loves you, just thought you should know.

***H**ey Satan,*

***I've got a question that I feel is best suited for you: What's the most entertaining way to get rid of my boyfriend?***

Dear idiot,

*Nothing* is easy when it comes down to dating or breaking up. And, though breaking someone's heart is already entertaining, there are many ways to do so. But first, let's talk about the number one reason for break ups: Dating.

**Dating is a period in which you collect enough "data" about someone, so that you can break up with them later and use that "data" against them.**

I once became some bitch's boyfriend just because she bugged me so damn much, had huge boobs and also because then I could later break up with her ass in a painful way. And by later I mean later that day, right after I got in her pants.

At first I liked her because her double lattes were large, but then she started nagging about me hooking up with her mother and so there it began.

I knew I could not be in a relationship that was only based on superficial faithfulness and exclusivity so I had to end it.

I took her on our first date to a strip club and broke up with her like we were on the set of *Jerry Springer*. Except I sent her a text message letting her know we were done while I walked out with a chunky stripper and her smoking baby.

**Oh, I was also smoking a Cuban cigar and laughing like a pirate while she cried watching me walk out victoriously.**

As you can see, this was an original way to get rid of that sperm vacuum I was dating. After all, it's not like I saw us blowing our 100 anniversary candles in the future. Plus she should have known that I like to play away from home before she let me put my pork meat inside of her.

Now here are some ways you can cleverly get rid of your boyfriend in an entertaining way:

1. **Fake your own death.** This is not just an entertaining and daring way to get rid of that someone special, but it is also a traumatic way to get back at family members for no apparent reason whatsoever. This is a win-win situation... for you only!

If possible, do it on your *own birthday* for more impact.

Once people discover you are not really dead, SUPRISE SURPRISE!, jump out of a cake and kill yourself for real right in front every one.

2. **Kill him.** Cutting your other half in pieces is always a good option. In the process of coming up with a good plan for your hopefully-not-first homicide, you need to remember that thanks to the Second Amendment you can own a pistol and even a rifle. This will help you to gun down Mr. Right at his front door while he is wearing his pajamas.

Killing is cool. I kill all the time, especially when I don't have to.

Killing is so easy, that sometimes I do it while I give myself a hand job. Oh, and remember, if the cops show up, kill them too. Don't let a perfect body go to waste, though.

Harvest his kidneys and other organs, throw them in a cooler and sell them the next time you go to Tijuana for cheap drugs or bad plastic surgery.

3. **Send him to jail.** To stage an innocent person guilty in a court trial could be as difficult as convincing a woman not to watch soap operas or talk about her feelings right when you come home tired from work.

However, with the right evidence, purposely placed in the right pockets, and false witnesses to back up "your version of the truth," you should be able to compromise your Adonis in a drug dealing case.

4. **Suddenly marry someone else.** Tie the fucking knot already, and at the same time show everyone that you are not breaking up with your boyfriend because of commitment issues.

Just think about all the fun you are going to have at your bachelorette party acting like a drunken loud slut. After you get married, wait a couple months and secretly get a job as a stripper.

This way you can be cheating on your new husband by deep-throating a bullfighter's meaty one-eyed in an alley.

5. **Get pregnant.** Nothing scares a man more than a pregnant girlfriend. New and exciting scientific insights have proven that pregnant girlfriends are another form of STDs and so are babies.

Pretend your water just broke as you inform him about this new life-changing event.

Then, don't have sex with him for a long time.

Tell him you have a headache, or your dog died.

Tell him it's against your new-found religion for him to put his beef in your taco, or that you can't because it's Tuesday.

Really draw this one out as long as you can.

Don't worry about you not getting any because in the meantime you'll be sleeping with his best friend.

While you're at it, sleep with his brother—heck, his boss, or that dude he carpools to work with every morning. If it has a dick, *jump on it*.

6. **Get amnesia.** It is time for you to grab the memory bat and hit your head until you get amnesia.

Have a big accident and forget who he is. Forget your own name and everything you used to know about him.

Then tell him you need some time to figure things out.

Either way, make sure you get a good head injury.

Finally, if after trying these tricks your boyfriend still won't leave, try turning him into a Cyclops by poking one of his eyes out. That should get the message through.

Best regards,

Satanico

# Family

***D*** ***ear Lord Beelzebub,***

***I have a confession. I am gay but I don't dare tell my family. They would judge me and my father would probably not talk to me again. But I want to tell them and come out of the closet already. What should I do?***

***Sincerely,***
***Rainbow Bright***

Dear Rainbow Bright,

I understand it must be hard for you to be a sinner in a world dominated by god and his ridiculous rules and prejudices. When I was growing up, I also had a lot of problems.

**I was insecure, introverted and I liked to do drugs and have sex with animals.**

When I graduated from junior high, I thought things would get better.

Then I became a successful lawyer and hired a beautiful and unlikely prostitute from Sunset Boulevard to bring along to various business events.

An attraction developed between us two, and I found it harder and harder to let the infectious ho go.

OK, this is not true. It is the plot of Pretty *Woman*.

Anyhow, stop being a fag and come out of the closet with your balls out and redecorate your parents' house with feng shui like all gays do!

I am sure they will figure out you are a pillow biter in no time and you won't need to explain shit.

Now I won't be hiding in YOUR closet.

Sincerely,
The Cloud on god's head

P.S. If you end up in a gay boy band, and want to use those last sentences in a romantic ballad, you have my permission.

***Dear Shamash the sun-god in Babylonia and Assyria,***

***I am pregnant again, and again I don't want to have this baby.***

***I have gotten a few abortions before and with no regret. But I was wondering what YOU think about abortion.***

***Truly yours,***

***Unavailable for motherhood***

Dear Unavailable for motherhood,

I think I am a fairly reasonable devil. I also know that I might not win something like the Nobel Peace Prize for what I am about to say. However, abortion is one of my biggest accomplishments with mankind.

**I sometimes want to sit on a mountaintop and yell to people all I have accomplished and how happy it makes me. But I don't because I know they would not understand.**

There are some things about keeping unwanted children that have kicked back for me though.

For instance, if you have a child you don't want to have, you both will suffer! You will raise your child in a wrong manner and with no love. This will also contribute to poverty since it will be one more mouth for you to feed and it will keep you both in misery. It's a win-win, but only for me.

What I am trying to say is that you have been a good follower for all your skanky, promiscuous and condom-free life and I am proud of you. Come to think about it, I don't think you should abort this time. You should have your bastard baby and be unhappy. Most importantly make *him* unhappy.

I still hate you, and yes, you will still burn in the lake of fire as I watch you from my fire-proof boat, but I'm still proud of you.

Bye baby (Bwah-ha ha),

SATAN

***Satan,***

***Well I don't know who else could help me with this other than God, and since I can't find his web site here it goes. I was on my way to being good but I blacked out drunk and the E was about to kick in.***

***Then my best friend's boyfriend and I thought it would be awesome to crash a hot tub, the first one we came across happen to be the holly water filled hot tub at the church down the street, which they use to baptize the local bible huggers…***

***I can't really remember anything that happened after that, but I woke up pregnant, does this make my baby Jesus?***

***Sincerely,***

***Mary Maybe***

Dear Mary Maybe,

I am sorry to be the one informing you that god is Internet-illiterate, and he has yet to acquire a blog.

However, you are in good hands. You don't want to write to someone who still tries to use signs in the sky like rainbows and shit like that to communicate.

I mean, even those feather-wearing, casino-drunken-ass, Native Americans who dress like Elvis while making s'mores and yelling hoo-ha around the fire in Vegas stopped making smoke signs and upgraded to emailing—though they still dress like Elvis and do shots of whiskey instead.

Not like smoke signs ever got them a reservation right? Get it? *Reservation*? Just kidding, they don't go to restaurants because they are too afraid of white people coughing on them.

**Anyway, conceiving a baby on drugs is as common as pigeons.** And staying on drugs until the time you actually give birth to your E-tarded baby is simply a trendy thing to do.

If you don't believe me ask Barbara Bush. This reminds me of the plot of a movie I once saw called, "Virgin Mary's Confessions."

When I saw this movie I popped a chubby beef so big that I was asked to leave the theater because no one else could see the screen. I just wanted to share that for no reason. Anyway, there is another little clarification I'd like to make about Virgin Mary. After having jesus, technically, Mary was *no virgin*! So please stop calling her "Virgin Mary."

If you suspect that your bearded fetus will turn into jesus and if that guy's name you fucked happens to be Joseph, then you might want to consider a drug-induced abortion in a foreign country.

It will only cost you $20 and a chicken. **After that, get an abortion every eight months even if you are not pregnant, just to be safe.**

You can never be too careful after fornicating in a filthy tub full of holy water. And you better get it.

Because if you give birth to another jesus, I am going to shove my fist so far down your throat that you will taste the deodorant on my armpit.

Burst in flames,

–SATAN

***D** ear Satan,*

***I am 10 years old and I want to make my baby sister cry, she gets all the toys and attention, what would you advice me to do?***

***Sincerely,***

***Sick of my sister***

Dear Sick of my sister,

You don't always undo a knot by simply pulling out one of the strings. Sometimes life's messiness requires more than that.

But first, you must ask yourself: *What is a baby?*

A baby is a tiny egotistical person who thinks we have nothing better to do than to comply with his/her needs. It is fair to say that if you try to talk to them you need to set your intellectual expectations on the low side, for babies are *very* ignorant.

Babies are famous for not knowing shit and lacking basic survival skills.

**I would even go as far as to say that they don’t even deserve to be called real people.**

Anything around them could be hazardous to them, so perhaps you can start by giving her a plastic bag to play with.

Tiny toys which she can swallow are also good candidates for her playground.

You could also break things around the house and blame it on her; make sure those things are some of your parents' favorite items. Maybe this way they start hating her as much as you do.

If none of this works, just go straight to your whiny baby sister and kick her ass and her toys too.

That will make her cry.

I’m hiding under your bed,

–SATAN

***Dear Cow of Wrath Damian,***

***My name is Skip. My wife Marie Blotch and I are Satanists, and we would like our new baby to have a satanic name. Can you please suggest any?***

***Also, how can we raise our children to be happy cowards?***

***Yours ardently,***
***Skip***

Dear Skip,

I didn't really read your letter but let's begin with an investigation:

Certain phenomena which are very frequent, such as turning your kids into happy cowards could start by having sex in your car with a hermaphrodite—while intoxicated and with your children watching in the back seat.

Although you may think this will not affect them pathologically, it might fuck them up *just enough.*

Now, given the fact that your name represents a style of gait, involving a combination of walking and jumping, I will do the suggestions for your kid's names from now on.

Perhaps a real Satanist name is in order, such as:

"Dick" Cheney, who by the way has served me more than you have. If not, here are some other names that you could use:

1. **Semyaz or Semiazaz**. Now *this* buddy of mine is a party and a half. We used to cruise Sodom and Gomorrah together back in the day.

If you got him drunk enough he'd teach you some dark magic, some divination—handy if you were gambling.

Sometimes he'd take a girl and teach her how to get a man so horny he'd nail anything that moved.

2. **Kokabiel or Kokba'el.** This fucker was a writer.

Lawyers used to come to him to get him to teach them how to fuck over their opponents. He came up with the idea of divorce.

3. **Armaros.** He was Kokabiel's buddy, and another demon lawyers came to. In fact, *he* was the one who came up with the idea of getting people to swear oaths, and then tempting them to fuck over each other, or making things happen so they couldn't keep their promises.

I can't even tell you how many wars he started and treaties he got people to break.

Good times, good times.

Now, if this seems like a lot of decisions to make, just remember, you can abort kids, even after they have been born.

I will re-baptize you in hell, Skip,

SATAN

# Society

***Dear Satan,***

***I don't get you some times. How can you be so angry about shit all the time? You know, all you need to do is smile.***

***Like, today, I was feeling pretty bad because the person I thought was my BFF asked someone else to be her maid of honor at her wedding. I was like, "seriously bitch? Who holds your hair back when you puke after a long night of drinking and cock-blocking? Who's the person who wouldn't tell you that you look fat so I don't ruin your self-esteem even before we wind up at a bar and at that point nothing matters anyway? You know who? ME! That's right, ME. And you go and choose some bitch who doesn't even know you gave herpes to half of the football team."***

***But anyway, I was feeling kind of mad about all that and I decide to go for a drive so I put some Fiona Apple on play to drown out my sorrow.***

***The sky was blue, the birds were out, I was having a good hair day, and guess what?***

***Everything felt better!!!!!***

***You boys just don't know how to deal with your needs and so you have to always fight and fart and whatever else it is you do.***

***Sincerely,***

***Trixie***

Dear STD-infected, pole strippin' abortion havin' Myspacing-whore—sorry, I meant Trixie,

What is it with you bitches and your shitty taste for music?

At what point do you start listening to shit like Journey?

Was it that after you turned 9 years old and you got your blossoming flower of womanhood that you discovered that your camel toe is actually called a *vagina* and then decided to let your period make all your stupid decisions for you?

**Seriously, if I hear another song by Fiona Apple I am going to rape myself.**

It's like the more retarded the song is the more you like it.

The more it makes you look and feel like a red-faced slobbering, lovesick cow in heat the deeper you think you are because you are in closer touch with your stupid feelings.

However, if you have to rely on a song to dictate how you feel, may I suggest this song I composed called "You are a Stupid Bitch and You Should Slit Your Own Throat."

I see skanks like you all the time blasting your Tori Amos CD's while menstruating on your way to the gynecologist with your fat loud-mouthed girl friends in the back seat.

This kind of shit makes me so mad that I always end up sucker-punching my own mother in the mammary. I know, you might have been thinking, "But Satan, why are you such a misogynist?"

However, you are not thinking that because you probably have never even heard that word and you don't even know what it means…

Anyway, women (especially young women like you), are stupid and your functions are very limited in life. These functions vary according —but are not limited to— your looks.

This is how it works:

Younger women who are good looking are good only for one single thing: Sex. **Oh wait, I didn't mean to limit you to that.** You can also be good for copulation. Or maybe monkey sex? Fucking?

Or… hmm let me think… *Sucking cocks for cigarettes!*

Anyway, if you don't agree, you are wrong, and you can take your pig tails and go play jump rope in the highway because you are a fag (independent of your gender).

Now, the function for ugly bitches is making the good looking ones look better!

Just notice when you go out and you find a group of chicks, it seems like the group gets progressively fatter as they walk through the door—**like as if a set of those Russian Matryoshka dolls were showing up to a mail order bride audition.**

This is because women are so insecure that they try to get fatter friends to hang out with them, so that they don't look like a piece of ham as opposed to looking like the piece of meat they really are.

I've also hung out with women over the age of 30, and that's no ray of sunshine either.

I went on a date with a 35-year-old hag the other day, this is how it went:

Hag: (Silence) + her blank stare = me wanting to take her purse to pay for my cab and leave.

Satan: Hey, why are you overly salivating and sweating like a fucking camel's asshole in the Sahara?

Hag: Blah blah… I am a woman of substance because I don't have the looks anymore which should make me smart by default… blah blah...

Satan: (YAWN)

Hag: Look, I can still be fun and clever… blah blah… I am so secure of myself… Please believe me!

Oh and I am not desperate to get pregnant THOUGH THIS IS BASICALLY MY LAST CHANCE!

Seriously believe me PLEEEEASE!!!… Seriously, I am NOT DESPERATE.

Satan: Hey, hag, I was going to tell you a compliment that was going to make your tits fall off but it looks like somebody beat me to it. Why don't you go and juggle your saggy tits so we can all become impotent in this bar?

Hag: How dare you?

Satan: Oh, look: my foot is up your ass already!!!

Hag: (cries) Wah wah!

Satan: (20 minutes later) ZZzzzzzzzzzzzzzzzzz, oh you are still here? SNORE.

Hag: Who am I kidding? I got a full generation of 20-year-olds to compete with and though they are stupider they still got their rack together…

Satan: Indeed…

Hag: (covers her face while crying on her way out…)

Reality hit her in the vagina, end of date.

Now, I know that many of the women reading this will soon start squealing and trying to argue my obviously correct points.

But don't waste your little neurons with your feminist arguments.

Feminism is nothing but the idea that women should be treated like children. **So put your bras back on,** go home, and fuck your worthless cats.

For instance, women think that menstruating is an excuse to be incoherent bitches just like a child would think that being hungry is a good reason to cry like a little pussy.

Being a woman has got to suck; in fact the only thing better than being a man is being Satan!

For example, women have more periods than a Morse code novel, which "affect" their stupid feelings, which brings me to my next point on the list:

Women have *way too many* stupid feelings.

**It's like every word you say to them becomes a civil rights movement against you.**

It usually plays out something like this:

Men: Hi, how are you today?

Women: Aaaaahhhh!!! Why are you so fucking instigating?

I am not a girl, not yet a woman! All I need is time, a moment that is mine while I am in between booo hooo hoo …….. (Extra periods) …….

Men: do you really have to stand in front of the TV to talk about this?

Women: You are such an asshole. You don't understand me, I wish you would have died when you were a fetus inside your mom's womb, you fucking piece of shit!!!
AAAAHHHH!!!

That pretty much summarizes how it goes…

Also, women can't tell the difference between good self-esteem and putting out for money. I don't even think I need to elaborate on this point because we all have seen them playing footsie with some old rich flaccid dude at tapioca time.

Another problem that women seem to have is that they don't even know what accountability is.

Case in point: let's say that a man who has a girlfriend gets really drunk at a bar and kisses another girl. If he was dumb enough to actually confess this to his bitch, he would say, "Honey, I am sorry but I got really drunk and kissed another girl, please forgive me." To which he would probably get his ass handed to him for being such an idiot and telling her.

But if a woman who has a boyfriend gets really drunk, kisses another boy and is confronted about it she would say, "I am sorry, babe, people kept feeding me drinks and got me drunk, and then this guy kissed me."

*Bull. Shit.* The stupid bitch decided to be a slut and deep throat some dude in a bar and will still not want to be held accountable, because women think that in life they can always get a do-over.

This double standard at their discretion is the kind of shit that pisses me off.

Thinking that because of their looks they can get where they want is what makes them earn 25 cents an hour less than a man!

What is it with expecting all this special treatment and yet wanting equality?

**Why should I put the seat up to pee and then down when I am done?**

Put it down yourself if you have to pee, bitch. After all, if you don't, *you* will be the one sitting on my processed Mexican beer. Talking about double standards, fuck all moralists of America! There's more hypocritical self-righteousness in this society than there is cellulite in a fat ass.

It's all over the goddamned place! For instance, women can talk shit about men and it is no big deal, it is supposed to be cute. But god forbids a man talks shit about women because he becomes an evil chauvinistic prick.

Or a black person can say racist shit and not be judged the same way a white person talking shit about blacks would be.

**Which is fucking stupid. Slavery is fucking over. These last generations have never seen a fucking slave so they can stop using that as an excuse to act like douches.** Anyway, now that I am done venting I might try your stupid advice and smile.

Burn in Hell, bitch,

–SATAN

***Dear Satan,***

***I'm 20 years old and I consider myself to be a rather deep intellectual individual. I know that 20 seems to be a young age for someone as worldly as me. Trouble is, I live in a small town in Texas where high school football is the big thing. Everybody's into barbecues and football.***

***I used to be on the cheering squad and my mother thinks I should just get by on my looks and marry some guy whose football career peaked in high school.***

***I think I should move to the big city, where I might find some deep-thinking artist to fall in love with, or maybe a philosopher or poet. What do you think? Where should I go? I don't want to live shallow for the rest of my life…***

***Jenny***

Dear Jenny,

Bitch, if you think "the big city" is not shallow and pretentious, you are about to get hit in the face by the shovel of disappointment.

But first we need to make some things clear:

1. **You are NOT an intellectual.** I don't mean to be the patty of reality in between your buns of delusion but I think you are confusing promiscuity and attention seeking with thought and reason.

Maybe if your pom poms were not so far up your ass you'd be cheering the chess squad.

2. **You are not deep.** So unless of course you are referring to your throat, calling yourself deep is the boner on the penis of incongruity.

OK, now that we got that out of the way, let's have a bite of the Big Rotten Apple:

Think of New York City as the vagina of the New World, and think of me as a giant gynecologist who knows exactly where the clitoris is.

Now, I know what you are thinking: "But oh lord of the darkness and trolls, I love vaginas!"

But then I would say with a Southern accent, "Oh yeah?

What about hemorrhoids?"

And then you would say "Hell no, I hate hemorrhoids, I even consider the word offensive."

To which I would reply, **"Well, in that case, think of New York as a giant hemorrhoid and think of me as a gigantic proctologist who likes to compare hemorrhoids with city landmarks to make clever little monologues.**

Then, you would politely agree with anything I ever say from there on.

Anyway, people in New York are not any deeper or intellectual just because they are in New York.

That would be like saying that Cubans speak English just because they are in Miami. Or that East L.A. belongs to Mexico just because there are so many damned people living under sombreros and feeding off leftovers from a piñata. Or like saying that Chinatown smells like garlic! Oh wait, Chinatown does smell like garlic.

Anyhow, if you move to the city you will find many levels of pretentiousness, way worse than those you will find in your stupid town.

For instance, you will find beautiful rich people with snobby pompous asses who think they are too good for anyone, and that they can shit cubes with their round assholes.

However, because of their beauty and affluence, their arrogance is justified.

Now, you are also likely to run into what constitutes the biggest population in New York City:

The Ugly Yet Pretentious Crowd! This type is sometimes harder to spot because most people are ugly in New York—especially hipsters, NewYoricans, Chinese, Arabs, Jews, blacks, males, females and *all* mammals.

Also, because no matter what season of the year it is, most people, men and women, dress like they are the Highlander, Duncan McCloud, their skin resembles Gollum's and their faces look like a fat loaf of ham. But the most annoying thing about them is:

Having to deal with their conceited attitudes and undeserved sense of self accomplishment—especially because *most* of them are nobodies.

The amount of people in New York who just sit there and look ugly is mesmerizing. I mean, there are so many ugly fuckers that they make Hell look like Hollywood.

**As a matter of fact, when I go out in New York and I meet girls, I don't know if I should buy them a drink, or shit on my hand and throw feces at them.**

Men are no exception; they all look like a fat clone of Daddy Yankee, with really fat ears.

**Seriously, come to NYC, hang out around 140th and Broadway and tell me if people don't look like an anus that is mad because it can smell itself.**

Walk in the subway and look around. People look like their thumbs got stuck in between their upper lips and noses right after they pulled them out of their asses.

I have seen third world countries' pederasts look like a sweet and fluffy piece of pink sugar candy compared to these ugly motherfuckers. No doubt a facial hairy mole attracts less negative attention to itself than an average looking New Yorker. I would rather be approached by a Mexican.

I mean, why do they have to look so fucking ugly? And how did so many ugly people end up living in the same place?

Ugly people are as abundant in New York as fat deformed retards in Alabama. What is it? The water?

The bad mood? Preservatives? Or maybe the immigration from the Dominican Republic and Puerto Rico? We may never learn the answers to these pressing questions.

Anyhow, for some reason they all have really high self-esteem.

It is probably a consequence of never having been anywhere else in the world (because NYC is diverse enough for them) to see the *real* standards that beauty goes by these days.

Women in New York don't know that the 80s are over, and most of them certainly don't know the term "waxing."

Or "tanning", "showering", "clipping", "hair combing."

Or "smiling" for that matter. And the men, well I have never really seen their faces because I am so distracted by how fat their ears are, but I'm guessing they just look like the fly in the urinal.

So if I were you, I would listen to your mom and marry some kid whose football career is peaking and stop fantasizing about poets and artist wannabes.

Die,

–SATAN

P.S. You will be the BBQ and the football in Hell.

***Dear Satan,***

***My body is that of a woman's: I have great big boobs and a fat ass, and I'm generally hairless, except for my head where my hair is long and luxurious.***

***I'm pretty damn hot. For a woman. But, Satan, inside me there is a big, burly hairy-chested, broad-shouldered, stinky sweaty greasy Neanderthal of a man just trying to get out. When I go out, I check out the women in their tiny dresses (and some of the more girly looking men too) and I wish I could walk over there and knock them out with my manly manly scent and drag them by their hair to my manly manly den where I can force them to fan me, feed me grapes and suck my… toes. I want to aim where I pee and fart with impunity. I want to whistle at chicks and make them think I'm god's gift to them.***

***I want to live in a house painted with poor color choices and with no cooking utensils. Satan, what advice do you have for a man trapped in a woman's body? How do I follow my lesbian calling?***

***Sincerely,***

***Barbie***

Dear Barbie,

After hearing your body description, I think I might get a big, burly hairy-chested, broad-shouldered stinky sweaty greasy Neanderthal inside you: ME.

I *love* girly looking lesbians. As a matter of fuck, I mean, as a matter of fact, if you look remotely close to what you just described, I would fuck the birth control out of you. Bitch I'd hit you so hard I'd dislocate your vagina. **Next time you have sex your squeezer will be on your hip.** Now if becoming a dick-less, male-looking sushi-eater is what you want, I can help you with that and here is how. However, it depends on your race to make it work better.

**If you are a white girl you need to:**

- Wear bi-curious accessories like unisex glasses, fedoras and Converse tennis shoes.
- Get the Ellen DeGeneres hair cut.
- Firmly strap your tits and put on a turtle neck to hide your boobs.
- Listen to retro or electronic music.
- In your conversations, use words like "equality," or "tolerance" or "entrepreneur."

•Put on some nonprescription emo glasses.

•Get a piercing in your lips or tongue.

•Neglect grooming. What's a stray mustache hair, or a zit? Throw some toothpaste or a Band-Aid on it and say you cut yourself shaving.

•Act pissed all the time especially to men (they are your enemy because they have a penis).

•Become an admirer of hipsters and advocate that they are creative and unique people though they all have unpaid fashion internships, act alike (like dip shits), and they all live in the same neighborhood.

•Walk around with an unjustified sense of masculinity and try to look as much as a straight guy as you can.

•Wear a tie every now and then.

•Read Anaïs Nin.

**If you are a black girl you need to:**

•Get cornrows.

•Wear army boots, really baggy jeans and a really long white t-shirt (inside the t-shirt put on a man's tank top).

•Get tattoos on your arms.

•Listen to lots of rap music.

•Use the "N" word and call other bitches, bitches. Oh yeah: by "N" word I don't mean "negligent."

•Act aggressive around other women so that they feel like you are a real alpha male about to bitch-slap them.

•Become a fan of Queen Latifah.

•Get used to not getting *any* pussy.

•Drive an Oldsmobile.

**If you are Hispanic or Middle Eastern you need to:**

•Keep your facial hair.

•Shave your head.

•Though you are a little man now, don't forget to take two hours to get ready like you did when you were a bitch.

•Wear wife-beaters.

•Use patchouli.

•Smile creepily and act overly protective when you talk to a girl even if you don't really know her.

•Change the spelling of your name to the gender-ambiguous form: Pat, Chris, Terry etc…

•Join the local softball team.

•Bite when you kiss to affirm to your partner that you have a bigger dose of testosterone than she does.

**If you are Asian you need to:**

Continue to act and dress like you do; all you really need to do is cut your hair off. Period.

Anyway, there are a few general tips you need to follow for you to maintain your manly reputation:

For instance, avoid getting pregnant as this will undoubtedly make you seem girly.

Sit with your legs open *all the time*.

Also, make sure you never wear panties, replace them with boxers and avoid using sanitary napkins as they are easily spotted.

You will also need to comprehend the art of the urinal.

This is not as difficult as it might seem, because when men pee in public restrooms they do everything possible to miss the actual urinal. Peeing outside the urinal is manly and easy.

Good luck getting some ass when girls realize that your penis looks like an open wound instead.

You will definitely need to get fanned in hell,

–SATAN

## ***Dear Satan***

***Why do you talk about women and treat them like they are just objects to play with?***

***We happen to be very important in society, and we've worked very hard to get where we are. But still you talk about us like we're inferior – even if we are capable of having the same jobs, or the same relationships that men do.***

***We may not have penises, but that's no reason to talk down to us. We are just as smart, and it's assholes like you that keep us women from gaining our proper place in society.***

***You and the men who believe in you, keep us down, and that's why the world is how it is. Grow up.***

***Angry Independent Young Woman***

Dear Angry Independent Young Woman,

If you ever watch *Sex and the City*, you will have an amazing insight into the female mentality and on why women are inferior.

For those of you who have never menstruated nor watched a stupid TV series starring women (besides porno), *Sex and the City* is a trendy show that rests squarely on a female demographic, which shows the vulnerabilities, anxieties and low level of intelligence of four independent American women in their thirties/forties in New York City.

**Basically, they are always bitching and nagging about how they can't get a boyfriend.**

I have never really seen it because I only do overly masculine activities such as putting a woman in between the washing machine and the dryer for a family portrait, but I heard they have horns and teeth in their sun-dried vaginas. And although they are in their "thirties," they are as wrinkled as my nuts after a three hour hot-tub bath. What really summarizes the female inferiority in this show is the way that these four "independent" women in their "thirties" in New York City want nothing else but to show their "independence" by getting a man who has his shit together to support them.

**These bitches go around like a fucking hurricane taking all the houses and cars they can.**

Now, I know exactly what you are thinking, "But Satan, why would they want a car so bad? The kitchen ain't that far!"

To which I would say, "I know, right?" And then laugh in an evil loud manner.

Anyway, though watching the Olsen twins develop was much more exciting, other women watch this show and think this is harmless fun.

But it isn't, this resembles the way they really see life. They become some kind of estrogen hobbit obsessed by a ring.

However, I have to admit that if women really acted like they were on the set of *Sex and the City*, things would be much better for men.

Just think about it, chicks would come to you and ask you out to dinner, then pay for it, fuck you until they squeal in such a high pitch that only dogs can hear them, and they will never call your ass back!

The day this starts happening I will turn into a piñata full of happiness waiting to be hit—though, even if you poured a gallon of straight rubbing alcohol into my dick to get it drunk, I'd still not fuck any of those nagging cows from *Sex and the City*. Not that I watch that show.

I used to date a girl like them. She was always menstruating on the carpet and talking about her rights and shit.

When she started wanting to be a blogger like Carrie Bradshaw, I had to replace her computer mouse for an iron and **teach her how to use the longest bone in the female body:**

**The broom.**

Here's the thing: feminism can get corny. You find the feminism stamp in a lot of things today: resentment and suspicion against males, the whole burned bras thing. It's very pop culture.

I particularly hate the feminists who get all new age/hippie and stop dressing well or shaving their armpits and getting all semantic, like "herstory," instead of "history." What the fuck, bitch?

**Proclaiming the superiority of your sex is not an excuse to let go of grooming, good hygiene or grammar.** After all, your flesh flower won't get any more superior because your armpits smell like you have been playing maracas all day.

What pisses me off the most is when young women who've never been treated badly by "The Man" start spouting resentments against men like they're being persecuted.

This is the same situation that happens with other minorities who blame "The Man" or "The Machine" for their failures, when in reality it's nothing but an excuse to fail.

Women get mad because even monkeys made it before them to the moon; however, they don't realize that the moon didn't need any cooking, sewing, laundry or vacuuming and if you don't like the reality of this you can sit on one of my horns.

Women use what many like to call "pussy power" to get to places in life. Oh sure, they get in for free in a few clubs, or drink for free on a ladies night, they might even get a job or two because of the high demand for poon.

Not all of them, since there are smart and fat chicks out there too. For this reason many women (especially in New York) think that they can play hard to get when they notice a man has the innocent noble intention of sliding his penis inside her snub-nosed vulva.

However, those privileges only last a few years.

Once they turn thirty some things change. Why?

Because women don't usually age as "gracefully" as men, or at least their aging isn't viewed as beauty in the male community.

When a woman turns thirty five, *usually*, their crack is not craved as much anymore, and they become replaceable.

Such false advantages don't teach women how to deal with the real world, until it's too late for them to confront it. For instance, some women tend to base their self-esteem on who they are with and not who they are. They say things like, "Oh I'm the doctor's wife," or, "I am married to a lawyer." Not, "I am a doctor!"

**Then, when the men turn 50 and start looking for a hot piece of ass to use them for their money the only meaningful relationships they have left are with their hairdressers, and their Chihuahuas.**

Of course, times have changed and many women out there want to become equal to men.

However, most of them only want this at their own discretion.

They want equality only when it is convenient for them. And god forbids they have to take the trash out or do real construction work—and no, sweeping the site does not count.

They forget that men discovered fire so that women can cook in it and make 25 cents less an hour while they are at it (unless they are Mexican women, in which case they only make 25 cents an hour).

Once I went on a date with a girl who tried to make me believe that men and women were equal and should be treated as such.

I laughed so hard I popped an hemorrhoid and jerked off to a *Cosmopolitan* magazine right in front of her.

**Then, I left her to pay the bill so that she would feel equal enough.**

Anyway, the biggest problem women have is: Other women!

Women act like a bunch of vipers against each other, they compete, PMS, envy and undermine each other based on a bunch of pretentious bullshit that they helped build around their social and psychological circles and even physical standards.

It's all sisterhood up in da club until one girl gets noticed and then the rest start cock-blocking like ninjas, trying to see who could be louder, drunker, sluttier.

As a man, if you get older, you become more distinct. But women as they get older, they have to compete with a bunch of young, hot-looking bitches that are after the same older man.

These standards don't usually apply to men, especially if they have money. Women tend to be more tolerant about a man's appearance than men are towards a woman's. Men can be fatter, older, smellier, or bald and women will still accept them. I mean even scum like cops get wives!

Men's love is unconditionally based on sex.

While women usually—and in the long run—search for love, men look for sex. Now let me ask you, **what is easier to get at the end of the day?**

**Someone who will love you for the rest of your life, or someone who will choke on your testicles?** I think the answer is deep inside your common sense. Oh wait. I forgot.

Women don’t have that! In which case the answer might be deep inside your throat.

Not only are women condemned to oppression by other women, but they are also weaker in many social aspects. For instance, emotionalism and sensitivity are qualities which women believe makes them special, like they could deal with the world in a better way because of it.

They defend this idea with arguments such as: “If women ran the world, there would be no war.” Oh yeah? Tell that to Margaret Thatcher, bitch.

The Falkland Islands didn't invade themselves.

Putting your emotions first doesn’t get shit done.

Men don’t do that. Women have so many little unnecessary emotions that it makes me want to punch rainbows and take a dump on a rose garden.

I mean it's like they upgraded from being bi-polar to multi-polar.

In many fields, including the job market, love life, and even sex, women have become replaceable.

Men jump from one woman to the next because other women make it possible.

**I mean, if there really was a great woman behind every great man they would just turn around, meet, and go for coffee.**

Often women come to me and tell me some little sob story about how I will be sad when I am old and have no wife to love me because I pork every piece of ass I find. But this is obviously a stupid little attempt to prolong their importance, as it is common knowledge that when I become 6,000 years old I will still be doing 19-year-old chicks, maybe younger. BAM.

Women are also organically inferior. They have periods, they get pregnant (yes that is a weakness) and they tend to be physically weaker than men as well as dumber.

For instance, I once sent my sister to get some coke and she came back with a Pepsi.

They also tend to be less talented, especially in music. It always has to do with something stupid like Mother Nature and New Age crap with flutes and chimes and a lesbian inclination, which can only lead to one thing as far as I am concerned: playing Satan's one-holed flesh flute!

So unless you want me to stare at your boobs while you give me your sermons about growing up, you are in for a disappointment, because the only thing that will grow up is my penis.

Do my dishes, shave your twat and shut it,

–SATAN

**D** ***ear Lord of Fire,***

***I am a woman; I am black, and also a Jew.***

***Any advice would be highly appreciated…***

***Sincerely,***

***Shabbatha Hanikua***

Dear Shabbatha Hanikua,

**Hold on while I wipe my ass because I just shit my pants.** When I hear about people like you, I wonder why people still think that god is merciful.

Not only he made you a Jewfican but he also made you a woman. I can't even imagine what your nose must look like.

I mean, how does that even work for you? Did you go to high school? Or did you get high in school? Did you ever get booked? Or did you actually read one?

Have you ever sprayed-painted the wall of a business or a school to then lean on it? Or did you go to business school?

Anyway, to navigate this crazy new world, you will need a guide to take your hand and walk you through life and to help you hang in there. And when I say hang in there, I meant a pole. And no, I didn't mean a stripper pole.

**For someone as special as you, I would recommend to end it all.**

Suicide is a mortal sin. See ya soon!

–SATAN

P.S next time you write, photocopy your boobs and send a copy.

***D** ear Satan,*

***I was sitting in class today, and a fucking dude came in wearing a skirt, at first I thought it was jesus that just showed his true colors but no, it was just a regular FREAK OF NATURE.***

***So I ask you, what can I do about him, or can you do something for me to have this disgusting human erased from this earth?***

***Thank you***

Dear Thank you,

Let me start by saying that your prejudices make me proud, and that aside from kicking his ass in the school's parking lot, you should only remember not to leave your kids with him.

A guy who wears dresses undoubtedly likes to rape stuffed animals and is likely to molest your family members even if he is not a Catholic priest.

Either way, he is a bitch who probably enjoys what women love doing, like nagging, standing in front the TV, taking showers with scent candles for inconsiderate amounts of time, eye-rolling, laughing excessively loud at unfunny jokes, crying, and having children.

Either way treat him like you would treat a woman and punch him in the crotch **then paint his nails in hot pink and wish him a nice period.**

Don't hold back,

–SATAN

***D** ear Satan,*

***I think it's an overall good thing that humans occasionally get eaten by sharks and bears.***

***Do you agree?***

***Bonus Question: Which actress would you most like to fuck right now?***

***-Bear***

Dear Bear,

Eating a three course menu of humans, boy scouts and tourists is one of the many functions of bears and sharks—especially if they are served with seared Maine oysters and Russian Osetra caviar or “Les Huitres ‘Pemaquids' du Maine Poelees au Caviar," as fruitcake-assed Frenchies like to call it.

**Bears love to eat humans.**

As a matter of fact, humans are to bears and sharks what track suits are to black people.

Except they eat them.

For this reason, bears and sharks are sometimes looked down upon—and so are black people, especially by overprotective pregnant mothers, who try to shield their stupid unborn children from everything the world has to offer.

As for what actress I am most likely to fuck, I’d have to say that being the hairy-chested devil that I am, **I would fuck any hot actress who lets me juggle her sweater stretchers.**

Cheers,
–SATAN

P.S. Unless you eat people too, signing as Bear is a non-verbose way of admitting you have a vagina.

***D*** ***ear Satan,***

***How art thou fallen from christ? I hope things are good down there.***

***I was wondering what you think about kosher food.***

***Sincerely,***
***An unhappy Jew***

Dear unhappy Jew,

For those of you who don't have rich friends and don't know what kosher food is, allow me to explain:

Kosher food is an invention of the Jewish religion that now is promoted by businessmen who try to become richer by packing it all up and putting it together on one aisle, **"The Chosen Aisle," for the convenience of god's "Chosen People."**

However, this separatist industry does not stop there.

Appliances for observing Sabbath rules can also be sold for the larger market. For instance, you can now obtain two sinks (one for meat and one for dairy), two conventional ovens and two microwave ovens, up from one of each.

Now to answer your question, I think kosher food is bullshit and maybe when your people stop running the World Bank you can come back and complain about the menu of people who can't afford to pay for expensive products. And if you disagree I will shove a Rabbi up your ass.

There is no Sabbath or kosher food in Hell!

Shalom,

—SATAN

***Dear Satan,***

***Why do all the bad artists in my town take themselves so seriously? I ran into a photographer today who blew me off because she was "working." I saw her photos and they sucked. Also, how much is my soul worth? I need some cash for drugs.***

***Sincerely,***

***Sonia***

Dear Sonia,

Daily life has changed over the last 150 years.

For instance, **now women have jobs that don't involve helping men get a boner**—though that industry has actually grown for a reason. Perhaps that is what women do best.

Although women are still required to put their breasts in their employer's hands to get a job, some of them still take it too seriously. Like this girl you are talking about.

She can't do a good job but she still wants to compete in a male dominated world such as photography.

When it comes down to photography, women should be only on one side of the camera as far as I am concerned, and that side is the topless side.

I guess many women still don't realize that competing with men can only end up in a miscarriage.

I once knew a pregnant woman who was trying to become "equal" with men in the labor world.

Her fetus was a man—a real man with hair on his fetus' chest.

When he heard what his mother was trying to do, he got so pissed off that he crawled out of her vagina and punched her in the fallopian tubes so that she would not have more kids. She was so afraid she ran to hide in the bathroom and cry.

Then he went and built a shed in the backyard and had a raw steak for lunch.

This is the normal reaction of men when women make stupid decisions like trying to be “equal.”

As for your soul… *that’s* already mine.

See you in Hell,

–SATAN

***Fight world hunger, eat a fatass!!!***

***Dear Satan,***

***I got a problem here and it's about fat people! You know what I am talking about, those fat people sitting next to you in a plane or in the bus!***

***They are always sweating and they stink! I don't know what to tell them every time they place their fat asses next to mine?***

***I also don't like little screaming and crying kids!***

***Everywhere I go those little bastards are getting on my nerves crying for something!***

***Should I buy a gun and kill everyone or do you have any better advice for me?***

***Also, are you fat? If so, fuck you too!***

***Yours,***
***Atomfried Bulletenfried***

Dear Atomfried Bulletenfried,

I share your hateful feelings towards the fat sweaty meatloaves. Sitting in a bus or a plane next to some flatulent lard that smells like potato puré is no fun.

$%&^%*&%$#%*34gkjfhkjf;66776dfgjhdghjghj 67843050&^*&^*((&*&)(*&JKJKYE %&Lkjcfjkgiugiug;ddddddfijkjwsw,,,,,dfgdfgdfh//sw

543894… Sorry. I passed out drunk on my keyboard, but I decided to leave it anyway because it looked like your name!

Anyway… as I was going to say before that shot of Jägermeister:

**Fat people should be eaten.**

They should pay for being so fat by being fed to the world's starving people.

The answer is: CANNIBALISM.

Think about it: About a billion people in the world are starving.

About 300 million people in the world are obese.

Just think of those porkers as another food source, send them to Somalia with a little salt and pepper *et voilà*! World hunger solved.

Most of them are probably going to come from the U.S., where two-thirds of the adult American population is overweight and obese, so you'll know they'll be well fattened up and have enough preservatives in them to last a couple weeks without refrigeration. And about those loud-mouthed children: feed them to the fat people, that'll take care of them. **And no, I am not fat; you burn a lot of calories in Hell pretty easily.** Anyway, you can go now and eat yourself to death and I'll see you in Hell.

Yours truly,
Satan

P.S. There is no Alka-Seltzer in Hell.

***Dear Rat of the Sulfur Sewer,***

***I am a writer but can't get published. Also, I have hemorrhoids.***

***Would you be so kind as to let me know what the next trends in poetry are gonna be so that I can go ahead and become a successful, pioneering author?***

***Best,***
***Pot Poet***

Dear Pot Poet,

For better or for words, when you write poetry you need to be more than observant, you need to become a participant of the gestures of life.

Painting with words, metaphors, and musicality—they are all rituals that have been developed over many years. It is difficult to come up with a new trend in poetry that doesn't come from an old one.

Plus when it comes down to poetry: Cursed be he who stirs my bones. Whatever that means.

**Anyway, what really matters is to have a good publicist and not how well you write. I mean, look at the Bible.**

So here is what I suggest to you:

1. **Get a literary agent**, someone who can help you sell your ideas.

2. **Stop smoking marijuana, and immediately upgrade to crack**—smoke it intensely and write down your thoughts.

3. **After a week of smoking crack ask yourself: Why simply smoke it when you can shoot it?**

Then say: Why not? Even better: write it down.

4. **When you write your poetry, remember to avoid moon/June rhymes.** Stay away from clichés (don't let your poetry turn into a sermon.)

Remember that adverbs and adjectives will weaken your poem.

5. **If all fails, take the James Frey route: lie, lie, lie about your experiences.** Blow up the smallest event.

Did a pretty girl look at you? Say you knocked up all the Playboy bunnies in a Wicca orgy. Got a splinter? Say you were crucified.

Don't give any credit to anyone else and make it seem to the world like you did it all by yourself. Lie to Oprah. By the way, James Frey is now a bestselling author, tops on the New York Times' bestseller list. Lying can be a lucrative business, just ask the Church.

Remember that sentimentality does not replace a feeling, and like Robert Frost said, “Verse in which there is nothing but the beat of the meter furnished by accents of the polysyllabic words we call doggerel.

Verse is not that. Neither is it the sound of sense alone. It is a resultant from those two.”

6. **Do something about those hemorrhoids.**

Maybe you can write them a poem!

Best regards,

SATAN

P.S Roses are red

Violets are blue

Sooner than later

I’ll come for you.

***D** ear Satan,*

***I think drinking and driving is fun!***

***I sometimes even snort cocaine off the steering wheel of my car as I take illegal U-turns while an under-age Thai prostitute gives me road head just for the hell of it.***

***The problem is that the police keep pulling me over at the slightest sign of intoxication. I feel like I am being discriminated against.***

***What to do?***

***Sincerely,***
***D.U.I'er***

Dear D.U.I'er,

Replacing your blood for alcohol without even using an IV to then drive around is as awesome as being a racist—or "hatecist," if you hate all races like I do.

This one time I had a few bottles of Chivas Regal and Jack Daniels with sulfured lava juice and a slice of lime on the side for breakfast... just for shits and giggles. **I was walking around like I was fucking Hulk or something, when I came across the intense need to piss on a homeless guy.**

However, I only found a tree at the Garden of Eden, and guess what was there? A naked chick, man!

So I gave her an apple while I was trying to impress her with my life-threatening dong, I mean I was all balls out and shit, man.

All of a sudden this long-white-bearded floating head came from a cloud and kicked my ass out of the garden. Can you believe that? Talk about injustice…

Anyhow, in your case this is what I think you should do:

1. **You should start a resistance group advocating for the rights of drunk drivers.**

Just think about it, alcoholism is a *disease*—a disease for which you are being discriminated against. You don't see a cop pulling somebody over for coughing or sneezing in their vehicle, do you?

So why inconvenience a victim of alcoholism who is trying to go out and find a job while exhibiting the symptoms of drinking? So make sure you prepare a group of valiant and violent men to join you in a riot.

Show up drunk for better effect.

2. **After kidnapping a few politicians' fat, red-faced, smelly children, demand better tests to determine your level of intoxication.**

Why should you walk on chalk and touch your nose like a fucking chimpanzee?

If these fuckers wanna have fun, they can go back home and buy a monkey.

These tests should be taken while driving, it's not like you are drunk-walking anyway!

You are drunk-*driving* for christ's sake!

They should just take the fact that you haven't killed anyone on that very night, which means you are good to go.

3. **Make sure you also riot for stoned drivers, as they are the safest drivers of all**—driving at a record of 10 miles an hour. And remember if you need to negotiate your hostage situation don't forget to wave your weapons in the air while threatening in tongues, just to stir things up a little.

They will just think you are so drunk that you are slurring your words; you should be just fine!

Now go out there and enjoy your cheap hookers and booze.

You will have a hair of the dog that bit you in Hell,

–SATAN

# Politics

***D** ear Satan,*

***How do you feel about gay marriage?***

***Marika***

Dear Marika,

Only god, his conservative mouth-breathers, and gays care about a stupid certificate that constitutes marriage. Marriage is probably the only way to get homosexuals to live a sexless life anyway so I don't understand what the big deal is. I mean, shit, it's a great way to get heterosexuals to live a sexless life, or rather, find a way to cheat on their spouses. **Just between you and me, anything that inspires self-righteous hatred is awesome** and gay marriage is just one of those perfect win-win situations: The Christian right will get their panties up their asses and spend time and money trying to wipe the scourge of gayness from the planet while their congressmen try to seduce male interns and solicit sex in public bathrooms...

I mean, really? I give them power and money and access and all they can do is wave their little wieners in a bathroom stall? **At least Bill Clinton had the right idea.**

Anyway, in the meantime, the gay community will hate the Christian straight idiots and that will lead to more intolerance!

I mean I know you have seen black gangs fight against each other; you have seen Latino gangs fight with others; white supremacist gangs have done the same and now guess what is coming out of the closet in gangs next?

I mean, jesus fucking christ, Marika (yes if jesus fucked christ that would be gay): you don't want to get gang-banged by a gay gang!

Ha-ha

Satan 1

christians and gays 0

Satan

P.S. In hell you will get fingered by ET.

***D** ear Lord of Flies,*

***I have way too much stuff to do and I think I work too hard, unable to commit the deadly sin of sloth.***

***I think I need a slave.***

***How do you recommend I get one and what kind is the best?***

***Signed,***
***Too much to do and not enough time***

Dear Too much to do and not enough time,

It sure is a difficult task to find time to do your own shit, even harder getting someone else to do it for you.

For many, slavery might be a sensitive topic these days, but it is something that has repeatedly happened throughout history.

This history has turned what we today call America—which is an incorrect term as America is a continent, not a country—into a melting pot.

**To keep it real, a melting pot that burns any other cultures that get in it.**

Anyway, there is something about slavery that brings people of the world together with charisma and megalomania across ethnic and national boundaries, allowing us to put aside our differences just to oppress other people *together*.

Now, before finding a scapegoat to pay so that you can enjoy loafing while being fanned with a giant leaf, you need to remember that picking slaves is not as easy as they make it seem in Alabama.

**First, you need to pound a bottle of whiskey and swallow a whole box of birth control pills for no apparent reason.**

Then, find a minority group in your neighborhood.

I know what you are thinking, but be creative… they can be midgets—*white* midgets—. You don't want to seem like you are committing an Obamanation with the whole political correctness we live with nowadays.

Keep it cool.

Walk right straight to your chosen slave habitat and proclaim yourself as their master and **demand they carry you home while their women hum songs with your dick in their mouths.**

However, be aware of any rebellious behavior in case they plan a revolution.

If they do and you are too drunk to escape, just dial... hum, 411... *Trust me...* someone soon will come to your ass' rescue...

There is no Pullin' a Palin in Hell,
–SATAN

***D** ear Satan,*

***Who do you think is the biggest public enemy?***

***Love always,***

***Amelia***

Dear Amelia,

Though the term "public enemy" has been incorrectly utilized to refer to awesome groups such as Satanists, rebel outlaws and rap bands, they are no enemies to the public at all.

The real sinister public enemy lies protected in the womb of society. And the rate of this danger gets higher and higher every day, kind of like gasoline prices, or your mom.

**Overpopulation is the *real* public enemy.**

I mean, women just won't stop vomiting kids out of their vaginas. It's like all they have to do is put their funny business on some man's nail-less finger and BAM! Bitch is knocked up!

All these kids are killing the world.

For instance, just think about these spoiled brats' *massive* consumption.

According to National Geographic's *Human Footprint,* there are more than 300 million people in America.

A child by age two and a half has already consumed 420 pints of milk, each pint having traveled 100 miles to get there.

During that time, each little shit has already used 3,700 diapers, which needs 1,898 pints of crude oil, four and a half trees, 715 pounds of plastic to manufacture, and this is just for milk and diapers for one stupid little child.

So just imagine the resources for the rest of their lives.

Listen women, having babies is not an accomplishment and it does not make you special.

*Everyone* is having them, how is that special?

Imagine how annoying it is to walk around in a world full of laughing children. They always run in circles instead of straight and they sing out of tune.

**It's getting to the point where you can't even masturbate in the back seat of the bus anymore**, because it's so full of stupid children not to mention the real people who stare at you. And everyone knows I can't masturbate when people are looking.

Just the other day I was on my way to the park, because it was a sunny Sunday afternoon and I wanted to find cute babies holding bunnies so I could stab them both, when this bitch that looked like Alf, because she was so damn old, got on the bus with five children. *Five*, like her presence there was not bad enough.

These infant delinquents were all running around saying hello to the people who were sitting behind them and they didn't even know them.

I'm pretty sure they were plotting to make the bus crash by yelling to the driver, "Faster, faster!"

Then, this little girl who was wearing glittery shoes (because she thought it made her look cute, but it didn't) was so loud, that I decided to wipe the windshield with her face and then shoved her back into her mother's asshole, which pretty much turned her into a flesh Popsicle.

The mother started bitching about something, I don't remember what.

**So I put her inside a cannon and shot her into a Planned Parenthood building that happened to be there** so that she would take some birth control. End of story.

I don't know what is wrong with people. Can't these morons see that the real public enemy is having so much public walking around?

Whatever happened to the times when you could torch things in objection to its morals? I say a child-clasm movement should be started and instead of burning books, burn children —though you can throw some Bibles in there too, just to get the fire started.

Then, take all the men who wear no condoms and cut their junk off so they look like a Renaissance statue. Cut arms too, just for the aesthetic twist.

Finally, nuke pregnant women. Either way you are all going to die because of your babies.

Love right back at ya, Amelia,
–SATAN

***D*** ***ear Michelle Wo– I mean Satan. Dear Satan,***

***You met Obama, eh? Well… Do you see a potential for Obama to take over YOUR position in society?***

***Anonymous***

Dear anonymous,

Let me set something straight, I did not meet Obama. Obama met ME! I know what you are thinking. "But Michelle Wo, I mean Satan, he is the president of the United States!"

To that I say, "Get a life before I demolish your ass with a 666-foot long pole, and put the American flag at the end!" For you to even speculate that the president of the United States Barack Osama I mean Obama could possibly take over *my* position in society makes me want to body-slam you against my trident.

I am superior to everyone. I am super awesome and shit.

How could you even question my position in society? **I am so fucking great that when I talk about myself I get so aroused that I drain my python right in front of everyone.**

As a final note, let me remind you that Obama is a president of a country only because I am the ultimate dictator of the world.

Vote for me,
SATAN

***D*** ***ear Mr. Satan,***

***What really constitutes a world leader?***

***Do you ever hang out with any of our world leaders?***

***Who are the craziest ones to party with?***

***What kind of alcohol does Obama drink?***

***Sincerely,***
***Monica L.***

Dear Monica L.,

**Mr. Satan is my father; you can just call me Satan.**

Something very important to know is that a world leader is a man who leads the world.

This is obvious to anyone who understands deductive reasoning. Leading the world is all they can think about, and if they would not lead the world, they would come to an end (the world leaders, not the world).

I attributed this world leadership to men only, because women are undoubtedly incapable of such a task. They are always shrieking about world peace and such nonsense.

**It's getting to the point where you can't even go invade the coast of a neighbor country without getting all these complaints from women and crybaby hippies who get their political world postures from smoking pot and staring at that Pink Floyd poster that has a triangle and a rainbow on it.** I of course do a fair amount of hanging out on the shoulder of most world leaders, like Hugo Chávez.

Fortunately, for them, I sometimes even write their confusing speeches.

When I do it, it goes a little like this:

Good afternoon prime ministers,

As you all see, I have mastered the essential craft of politics in this chamber. I have also spoken about free trade; subsidized and nationalized the moral authority with legitimacy of the negative equity that services this interest's condition.

As a consequence of my captaincy and pathologically reinforcing of the productivity of the monarch commission and grand coalition, I lectoralcalculated the labor intrinsically passerelle as you all well know.

Thank you. (Clapping…)

You see? That's some United Nations shit right there.

That same old speech! Now when it comes down to partying with these confetti-throwing celebration beasts, there is something really important to obtain first: Diplomatic immunity.

Diplomatic immunity is essential to get a good-old-break every time you are linked to a cocaine habit, or every time you receive accusations for immoral behavior.

Now Monica, you are the Paris Hilton of politics, and you should know a little about this topic since you are incapable of not taking a congressional whiskey dick and putting it in that hole on your face.

I got a pretty ambitious line of Arabic businessmen who would love to hang out with you.

This reminds me of this one time I was hanging out at my married friend's house, and I accidentally walked into his wife while I was masturbating.

In this case, diplomatic immunity could not do much for me, as my friend and his wife have never called me to hang out again.

Anyhow, back to your questions. The craziest world leaders to hang out with, which by the way, you indisputably could polish their door knobs are:

1. **Nicolas Sarkozy.** This French bastard is one of my favorite political figures. I mean this guy bangs models and shows up drunk to press conferences. He is so cool I think he should have his own character on Grand Theft Auto.

2. **Vladimir Putin.** At first he might seem a little hard and stiff. Like the nipples of a blind lesbian in a fish market.

He gives you an impression of contained power and a stare that shows no emotion.

However, this son-of-a-bitch rocks out with his testicles in the air to the tunes of Tchaikovsky and a bottle of straight Popov down in the woods of Moscow.

3. **Bono.** I know what you are thinking, "But Satan, Bono is not a political figure! He just likes to suck giant hard ones." To that I say, you are right Monica, you are right. *My bad.*

4. **Pope Benedict XVI.** Any man who wears in public a dress and a crown that looks like a pointy party hat is definitely a pedophile. And nobody in the ass-embly of god parties like pedophiles.

I know you might be thinking that he, just like Bono, is not a political figure but you are fucking *wrong*.

This ally of mine has been manipulating the relationship between Church and State since the beginning. **So if you want a party full of bling bling and wine, and prostitutes and AIDS, you know where to go.**

Finally, about Barack Obama's favorite drink, he likes wine (a.k.a. grape juice). Surprise Surprise!

Hasta la victoria,

–SATAN

# Religion & Existentialism

***D** ear Satan,*

*I think my hamster is possessed by you. He bites me all the time, attacks the side of his cage when I walk by and on one of his recent escapes I found that he had cornered my dog and was foaming at the mouth.*

*If you are possessing my hamster, would you please stop? If you aren't, would you suggest changing his diet or something?*

*Sincerely,*

*Covered in hamster bites*

Dear Covered in hamster bites,

Hamsters are inexpensive and common household pets.

These rodents are friendly and fairly easy to care for because of their small size.

However, when they are possessed they are rather turbulent.

**Now if you stop playing Satanic music backwards and invoking spirits of insurgence and chaos while waving your horn-gestures in the air and mosh-pit dancing with your red-blooded eyes while screaming O Lucifer, Son of the Morning in front of your hamster, then he might stop being possessed.**

However, if nothing else works, you can also try a seed diet and see how that goes—pelleted rodent rations that contain from 18 to 22 percent protein are suggested for feeding hamsters in captivity.

Many hamsters prefer sunflower seed-based diets to pellets, but these seeds are low in calcium and high in fat and cholesterol.

I once had a pet like that and it was I-N-S-A-N-E. It was covered in tattoos, enjoyed casual drug use and tried humping other species.

I lost him in Vegas one day, while I was getting my speedo line waxed. Anyhow, hamsters are not going to be the *only* thing biting you when you get to Hell.

See you in my cage,
SATAN

***Dear Satan,***

***I have a question about you and your relationship with god.***

***I would say that after my thinking I feel very much disappointed. What about the dichotomy you have with god and the good side of things? From someone as smart as you say you are (to seduce everybody with temptations and bring darkness everywhere) I would expect much more than a "black or white" (you or god) kind of thinking.***

***Dichotomist thinking shows no intelligence on your side.***

***After all when people feel good they say they are in "christ" but actually they are just enjoying one of several sins (sex, food and all pleasurable things…)***

***My point is that both of you are the same (same crap). Bullshit in hell or Christ.***

***Nobody believes in that division anymore anyway.***

***You have to give us something better that that… if you are capable, of course…***

***the always skeptical***

Dear the always skeptical,

Although your argument was ineloquent and hard to understand, you said, "My point is that both of you are the same (same crap). Bullshit in hell or christ."

This is a contradiction of dichotomy. As dichotomy suggests, god and I have a mutually exclusive nature between good and evil. Like the yin yang. Now you are implying that we are the "same crap" which, as I interpreted, puts us both (me and god) as negative or evil entities—**in which case I *win* and god lost *again*.**

I hope this helps you figure out what a sad motherfuckin' fallacy your argument was.

Now both I and god hate you!

You are fucked,

SATAN

***D** ear Satan,*

***If god created the world and all the life within it, then who created you?***

***Sincerely,***

Dear Anonymous,

The real question here is who created god? I don't claim to be the creator of anything besides Cinemax, Democrats, public transportation, Camel lights, hipsters, feng shui, mildew, chess, Somalia, undergrad idealisms, and Washington—though I've never met anyone from Washington, I'm not even sure that place really exists. Anyhow, god's origin is what should be in question. Just think about it: he is all like, "Oh look, read the Bible. It has all the answers for everything in it." And then, once you read it, you have more questions than you did before you read it, **kind of like when you try to analyze Fiona Apple's lyrics. I mean, was she raped? Or did she walk in on someone who was masturbating?** Right? Right!

Bwah haha,

–SATAN

***Dear Satan,***

*You ever feel that whatever the fuck it is you are doing is the most boring thing in the world? Here I am, in perfect Paradise. And across the world, all Hell is breaking loose.*

*I mean seriously. The Philippines, Samoa, Indonesia? The Ring of Fire? What kind of party are you having out there? Why wasn't I invited?*

*Here in Paradise it never gets too hot. Not really. It's never too cold. We had an earthquake almost a century ago. So I'm sitting at the beautiful beach in the beautiful weather, looking at the beautiful water. It doesn't mean shit.*

*All I can think about is death and destruction: people drowning in floods, getting sucked out to sea, buried under landslides.*

*I should be thankful that god put me here. This is what everyone wants.*

*People think I'm living the dream. But this isn't my dream. I want something else.*

*Satan, what do I do? How do I make my life mean something?*

*Eve*

Dear Eve,

Penis, penis penis penis, penis penis penis penis penis, penis penis penis penis, penis penis penis penis penis, penis penis penis, penis penis penis penis penis, penis penis penis penis penis, penis penis penis penis penis, penis penis penis penis penis, penis penis penis penis penis, penis penis penis penis penis, penis penis penis penis penis, penis penis penis penis penis, penis penis penis penis penis, penis penis penis penis penis, penis penis penis penis penis, penis penis penis penis penis, penis penis penis penis penis, penis penis penis penis penis, penis penis penis penis penis, penis penis penis penis penis, penis penis penis penis penis, penis penis penis penis penis, penis penis penis penis penis, penis penis penis penis penis, penis penis.

**The ring of fire will be your ass hole with so much motherfucking penis,** penis penis penis, penis penis penis penis penis, penis penis penis penis, penis penis penis penis penis, penis penis penis penis penis, penis penis penis penis penis, penis penis penis penis penis, penis penis penis penis penis, penis penis penis penis penis, penis penis penis penis penis, penis penis penis penis penis, penis penis penis penis penis, penis penis penis penis penis, penis penis penis penis penis, penis penis penis penis penis, penis penis penis penis.

Getting jiggy with it, byotch,
–SATAN

***D** ear Santan*

***Santa***

***Sata***

***Satan***

***Is Santa Claus for reals?***

***My mom says if I good then I get presets from him. But my frend Ari says Santa Cauls is not for reals. I want presents! Jesus dos not give me presents if i'm good but we go to church every week and I have to dress nice and be quiet and not make farts. Wat do I do, want presents!!!!***

***Bambina***

Dear Bambina,

I know that it is hard to believe that someone who lives in a land of perpetual snow, works one day a year and eats reindeer could exist, *but just look at Sarah Palin*.

I admire how you question what your mother tells you.

However, this time she is right and your stupid friend Ari is wrong. Santa Claus does indeed exist.

Now, I know what you are thinking: "But Satan, how can that fat ass shove himself through a chimney?"

**But that has a perfectly logical and rational explanation: Santa does Voodoo.** But that's not all of it; there are a few things you might need to know about him before observing Christmas.

For instance, Santa has a list of boys and girls from all over the world, and like that is not creepy enough; he categorizes them into "good and naughty."

**If that does not raise a red flag on your pedophile radar, you can hug Rudolf's balls with your mouth.**

Though to be honest, you'll probably enter the "good list" that way—or by sitting on Santa's lap.

He is, after all, the patron saint of prostitutes.

Anyway, the reason why Santa has this separatist list is because he believes in racism and discrimination, (as should you). For example, you don't see Santa riding over Central America to drop gifts too often, do you? And you don't see little Somalian kids expecting a fucking pony for Christmas, *right*?

As a matter of fact, Santa went to Africa only once in his career. When he was there, he asked if the kids had been good and ate all their vegetables—when he found out that they didn't (because they had none) he took off with all the gifts.

Another reason why Santa Claus is an asshole is because he significantly determines the standards by which kids have access to Christmas through his judgmental views on your behavior. His multibillion-dollar enterprise controls the monopoly in the toy industry, enriching himself from a celebration that has no shit to do with him.

He also enslaves midgets who work for him in the North Pole (or Northpole for short).

These little cupcake-ass midgets don't have other jobs in the area because Santa's sweat shop took over all local business.

Now they are forced to work and be exploited for his corporation while Frosty the Snowman melts from the global warming Santa's factory creates.

Have you noticed how stores open at 4 a.m. after Thanksgiving making people think they have to be out there before anyone else to get better stuff than everyone else?

**That's what adults call "materialism." And what Santa calls "Christmas."**

There have even been reports of Santa delivering deathly toys, so if I were you, and I see that major- league fat dipshit coming down my chimney, I'd bust up his shiny jingle bells so hard that we would both scream.

I mean, unless you want your own balls hanging over the chimney like stockings after your brand new Mattel's Missile-launching Colonial Stellar Probe® explodes in your face.

Santa is pretty much a Nazi. So don't get ensnared by Santa's claws. He is out there creeping in the dark around your house **and for Christmas he is going to bring you a big black robot called Bonertron who is going to play hide-the-rocket in your anus.**

So, if you want presents for reals, I got one right here for you. It's a 43.21″ inch US M1903-A4 sniper rifle for you to wait by your chimney with and do some reindeer hunting.

Merry Christmas, Bambina,

-SATAN

P.S. In hell, during Christmas it snows black ashes.

***Dear Sire of Fire,***

***The mother of my roommate will not shake hands with me because I am a "stranger." That's what her religion teaches her. Can you share with me any advise as to how the fuck to deal with these mindless religious types?***

***Only waving,***

***Handshake-less in Baltimore***

Dear Handshake-less in Baltimore,

When you come across a bias that may be religious, it's time for you to put on your "Oh Shit" gloves and leave no fingerprints behind.

Perhaps a Congolese-style militia operation against your roommate's mother and her religious group would cease the conflict? It kinda works in the Congo and even the Middle East if you take the civilian cost out of the picture.

**Just ask the fellows at the United Nations, they should have some pointers on how to look the other way.**

All you probably need is a large stash of weapons, ricocheting bullets, people bleeding out and probably some looting. Then just go for the usual turmoil.

Or you could disguise your house as a church, lure them in with fake promises of free communion and a cappuccino machine and then bust a cap on their ass.

What are you waiting for? Don't be passive-aggressive. COMBUST THEM!

On your way out try to ruin the shit out of the Bible Belt states.

However, don't blow your hands off; you may end up handshake-less forever.

Peace and Love,

–SATAN

PS. You will probably sit on a mine in Hell.

***D** ear Satan,*

***If you were to compete against jesus on a skills' contest what would you do?***

***I imagine jesus walking on water, making blinds people see, paralytics walk, coming back from dead and even giving Maria Magdalena the best fuck ever.***

***Please my Lord, don't disappoint us! What would you do to beat jesus?***
***With all my heat!***

***Your biggest fan***

Dear Your biggest fan,

Competing is something I have done from the very beginning. And by "very beginning" I mean Genesis, a time when, by the way, sweet baby jesus was not even born.

Though redefining success is usually the main key in winning a competition, *I* don't even need to do that when it comes down to competing against jesus.

You may be thinking, "But Satan, what really is important is to compete and not to win. Grow up!"

But then I'd say: "No. You grow up!"—which will make you feel immature, because after all, *you* started it.

Anyhow, from the very beginning, I have shown my competitive spirit in many ways.

For instance, **I created darkness before god created light.**

**I came up with seven sins before god came up with the Ten Commandments and so on. Even after he created the Ten Commandments, I created thousands of stupid laws that rule today's governments.**

For example, if you shoot somebody's dog in Nevada while on their property, the law allows them to hang you.

Also, you are not allowed to commit murder wearing a bullet-proof vest in New Jersey.

However, you are allowed to legally beat up your wife as long as it is on a Sunday morning on the steps of the state house in South Carolina.

Nevertheless, my competition skills do not stop there.

When sweet baby jesus was born I still ruled the ring.

I remember this one time I was walking around, minding my own business.

When suddenly sweet baby jesus, who was about 12 years old at the time, came out of the synagogue and started sticking his tongue out at me, so I shoved him into a camel's ass.

**This is why you don't hear about jesus in the bible again until he was like 30.** He was in the camel's ass *all along*.

I have always competed in all aspects of life.

Not just religion, but also politics, law making, society and more. You can see examples of my doing in almost every aspect of society. I can also tell you that jesus walking on water and shit, would not even compare to me having sexual intercourse with Mary Magdalene. I mean, c'mon, she was a ho, and I've got three horns!—which is officially an orgy.

Magdalene would have needed physical therapy and counseling after a sustained session of me boink-festing her with my thrill drill. (Not to rub it onto jesus' face but *I*'ve got the biggest urinal unit.)

First place: SATAN.

Second place: SATAN's magnanimous genitals.

Third place: Mary Magdalene.

Cheers, fan,

–SATAN

***D** ear Satan,*

***What practices do you recommend for hell-lovers? I mean, Buddhists meditate to reach the state of illumination, Catholics pray their way unto christ, I am not chosen like the Jews who… well, I don't exactly know where Jewish go after death and what do they do to get there. Maybe you can tell me?***

***The point is that every religion has its methods to achieve their ultimate goal (having a nice time after dying). What will be the equivalent of illumination for us sinners? Which are the steps to get there?***

***The always confused***

Dear The always confused,

First of all, you do not need to be a Hell-lover to get into Hell. The paradoxes and inconsistencies of religious practices will get everyone into Hell.

You should not be too worried because I make it pretty easy to come to Hell—unlike god: **he makes getting into heaven harder than a cholo at a quinceañera party.**

To enlighten you a little bit about your doubts on Jews:

Their theology, rituals and practices are not any deeper than Michael Jackson's voice or taste for children's corn holes.

Most of their shit was actually *stolen* from ancient books.

Just like in the farce that is Christianity and Catholicism, the Jewish theistic history comes from a mix of polytheistic myths and legends from assorted cultures, which they have adopted (plagiarized) to generate a monotheistic doctrine.

These stories are as sporadic as a Mexican's beard.

For instance (get your air quotes on), "Let there be light" was taken from the Theban creation epic—which is as boring as the Bible.

Adam and that slut Eve were "inspired" from the Egyptian Geb and Nut, just like their retarded "chastisement and loss of immortality" was "taken" from the Mesopotamian story of Adapa.

The twelve tribes of Israel, just like the twelve dumbass disciples who **walked around like they were the fucking Power Rangers**, were based on the twelve signs of the Zodiac.

The *Ten Commandments* were also "inspired" in the *Code of Hammurabi* though in this case the Jewish Yahweh replaced the Sumerian sun god Shamash and so on…

The ultimate purpose of their teachings was to give the Jews an excuse for not shaving their smelly beards, a special separatist status of "god's Chosen," and to spoon feed pacifists with a meek slave-like mentality that has helped the Church gain domination over the State through fear, utilizing the media and Matisyahu to control the masses.

Now, I don't really know but maybe their disproportionately large noses have something to do with whether or not they will enter the "Kingdom of god" or wherever they go when they die. I think that if there is something they should circumcise it's their gigantic noses. BAM!

Anyway, don't be down because you are not a "god's Chosen." You know what they say, **If life gives you lemons, fuck lemons and drink irresponsibly** (I'd suggest Tequila shots, that way you can take those lemons). Anyhow, concerning how to reach a state of illumination for a sinner, the answer is obvious. Sin and sin a lot! Abusing drugs and alcohol will also help you focus on achieving your sinful nirvana.

Remember that blacking out drunk while driving with your family in the car is the equivalent of illumination for sinners, so let the rest of your life begin now and forget about all that stupid seat belt nonsense.

See you later, sinners,

–SATAN

***D ear Ball of Smelly Yak Fur,***

***I am a Buddhism. I learned my religion in Tibet; a place, by the way, where you and all the rest of your Christian coterie do not exist. That's right, Beelzebub: you are nothing but an idiotic christian notion with no relevant existence elsewhere.***

***I live in wisdom that is not self-centered; I do not expect retribution for my good or hell for my sins, so please take that biblical oven of yours and shove it!***

***God, I can't wait for Tibet to be an independent nation again and shed its peaceful light all over the world. Buddha is smiling while you are full of hate. Who's the smart one now?***

***Not yours,***

***Disciple of Laughter***

Not so Dear Disciple of Laughter,

**If I don't exist, then who the fuck are you talking to?**

Anyway, when you ask, "who is the smart one now?" after you said that you are "a Buddhism," is like hearing Ronald McDonald ask "who is the clown now?" after saying that he is "a hamburger."

That's a fucking laugh riot right there. **Would you like a McFuckYou with that?**

Though you probably meant to say that you are a Buddhist, my example resembles Buddha better, because he obviously ate a lot of junk food and looked a lot like a special kid who suffered of heavytitis.

Anyhow, you argue that I am part of a Christian coterie whose existence is irrelevant elsewhere.

However, all elements of Buddhism were taken from pre-existing ideas from India, just like Christianity and Islam, and there share very relevant similarities that warrant my existence by default.

On the other hand, the compiled stories from Buddha were written by multiple people and no aspect of Buddhism is other than what you'd expect to find in early India.

**In short, it is entirely possible that there was no Buddha and that the stories of the Buddha's life were merely the same stories of similar lives of other sages, given a new catchy name.**

Just like the Bible (a book that is known to be true, just because it says that it is) talks about jesus. And even worse, it teaches that the second coming of jesus will be better than the *Return of the Jedi*—like that's possible. I think god probably forgot to read my version of Genesis, called Genocides.

Now that's literature.

So anyway, answer this question: If your imaginary friend thinks that YOU are imaginary, do you still exist? Oh wait: that might make you a Scientologist, I'm not sure.

Either way, if Buddha did exist, he was a fat ass who thought he was in Nirvana—though Kurt Cobain told me he has never met him.

Yet his followers keep teaching his religious postures after he put himself in a coma through meditation or he ate his meditation or something like that.

This is exactly how they invented comic books and religion: **Some old guy decided to teach about something he knows nothing about. It's like shitting something you didn't eat.**

Here is one good comic book/ambiguous religious idea (just like Tibetan Buddhism) for you:

It's about two super gay heroes called, "Butt-man and Rub-in."

They're a dynamic duo that wears their underwear over their pants, while being up against the evil forces of slyly seductive but highly toxic vaginas.

Take that, jesus and Superman!

Now, getting back to your question, you said, "I live in wisdom that is not self-centered; I do not expect retribution for my good or hell for my sins."

However, I find this also to be untrue.

Buddhists believe in Karma, and Karma is a way of summarizing the selflessness which arises from all the actions one makes throughout one's life.

Your heaven or Hell is summarized in the concept of reincarnation.

As you might come back as a king or a cockroach, you do expect retribution that is self-centered as you look out for your own well-being.

**Which is kind of stupid because you are going to Hell anyway, just think about it**.

You don't believe in god, so he doesn't like you.

You are also screwed with me because I find you to be a pompous ass motherfucker who won't eat a cow but wears pretty nice leather sandals.

Which is also stupid since even god likes it when people kill animals—especially if they sacrifice them on an altar to his name.

Anyhow, this means you will end up in hell, with a flaming 300-year-old bonsai tree up your ass, while I give you a Chinese drunken master roundhouse kick to the testicles.

**You might as well pour gasoline on yourself and set yourself on fire in protest already.**

You also said that you can't wait for Tibet to be an independent nation again, or some Jackie Chan ching chong shit like that.

However, Tibet barely has the minimum requirements of a state society, since international recognition of a state as such is a primordial aspect of a state's existence.

Tibet as a state has a specific history outside of Chinese occupation that can count for its unity and particularity, but its lack of independence in the international arena makes its definition as a state problematic.

One needs only to remember that Puerto Rico is also a state society, but internationally it is only an associated state within the larger U.S. federal system.

So take all that Brokeback Mountain peace speech and shove it up your pooper before I UFC you.

Perhaps an old Tibetan song would fit Tibet's reality:

"The sky is turquoise, the sun is golden,
The Dalai Lama is away from the Potala,
Making trouble in the west."

Fuck you,
–SATAN

P.S. What's the point of Tibetan women shaving their heads when their birth canal is so bushy you could hide a microwave in it?

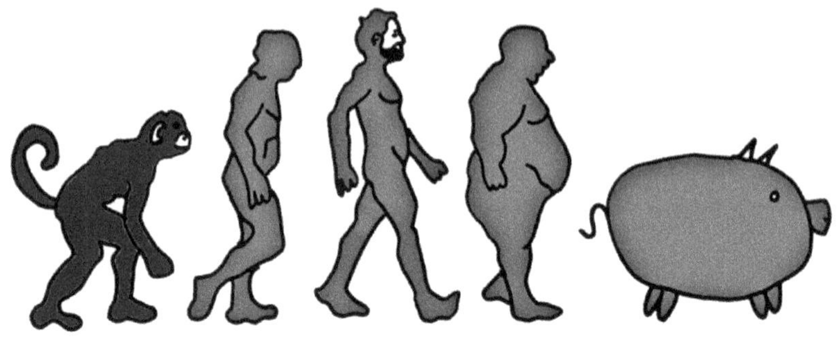

***D**ear Satan.*

***My name is Burt and I am a high school student from Illinois.***

***I believe that God is all good and all powerful. But I am very confused about the origin of humans and what my theist perspectives should be. At my church and my Christian High School, some teachers talk abut how God created us and the rest of living things, but other people tell us that we came from a fish (what the hell???). I am very confused, how are fish, God, and I related to each other? Could you enlighten me please?***

***I hate school***

***Burt***

Dear Burt,

I will enlighten you, alright.

First thing you need to know, is that "abut" is actually spelled "about"—it is obvious that you do indeed hate school.

Second, I want you to think about this: Nature seems to summarize the whole theory of evolution in a nutshell and you could tell this to your Christian teachers next time they harass you with all that theist nonsense. **These Christians know everything about farting, but in the end they don't know shit.**

When you are conceived, you live in salt water for nine months, just like the theory of evolution suggests you did as a fish in the ocean.

In the womb you start developing into other forms that follow the suggested perspectives of evolution (which, by the way, are disgusting).

There is evidence of what could have been gills, and the vestiges of a prehensile tail, as the fetus develops in its mother's womb.

This explains why babies are so ugly and come out looking like lizards.

Even before babies can walk, they can swim and for many babies the instinct to hold their breath and swim underwater is stronger than it is in older children and adults.

Anyhow, when you get pulled out of your mother's bearded slimy slough of a taco, you can't walk yet, so you get around the same way primates (or women who want to succeed) do—on hands and feet, climbing and crawling until eventually you stand erect and walk on your two feet (and by erect I mean straight, and by straight I mean properly positioned).

Hopefully, you develop into a modern man—though most of you people act like apes that enjoy shitting on their hands to salute others... though that's not really how apes say hello.

Now, about what your theist perspectives should be.

I've got to tell you that believing in god is harmful and a bad idea for you and for society.

I mean, just look at what happened to Noah in the old book when jesus beat him up and took over the Old Testament. Hah!

Didn't see that coming? Me neither.

Anyway, one of the reasons why I think this way is because religious people tend to attribute morality to a desire or command of god knowing that, for humans, morals can be rather fragile.

Like when a priest slips and falls with his dick inside an innocent child who was bending over inappropriately.

**The problem with this is that people take those morals or values from something outside of themselves and for that reason they are not fully accountable for what they do, as everything is attributed to god's will.** And in that name there springs anything from simple lies, to my personal favorite, genocide.

Now, not that I am playing devil's advocate here (because I am the Devil), but I don't see religion inspiring moral behavior. Just ask my buddy Osama Bin Laden.

Perhaps unhitching the metaphysical and divine from your everyday life will be much more beneficial.

That way, you can just start experimenting with drugs and unprotected sex instead.

You might be thinking, "But Satan, how can religion be bad?" to which I would reply by punching you with my permanently engorged cock in the face because I just explained that.

So, sorry to be the one to tell you—but someone has to pull that monkey out of your ass: **There is no cosmic force to distribute justice. PERIOD.**

Plus the idea of this suffocating presence paying attention to every time you arm-wrestle your Cyclops is a little oppressive.

Religion is a corrosive idea.

I mean god, c'mon! When I bake cream cakes I don't want to be stared at.

Emptying the banana is "me time."

Now, I know that there are many arguments out there for the existence of god. And that you probably are thinking, "Hey Satan, if there ain't no god then there ain't no Satan."

However, you can five-finger-humpty-hump-love-pump my dong because that is a double negation and you make no sense.

Hah. Satan 1 - Ebonics 0.

There are also people who argue that anything that has a definition (which god does) indeed does exist.

Now god's definition is "greatest conceivable existence," and logically, by this definition, this should mean that god exists.

However, this is like asking Wile E. Coyote how to catch the Road Runner.

**Because if you look at the definition of unicorn you will see that it is a horse with one horn on its head, which lacks existence, and yet has a definition, showing that the definition theory is bullshit.** And if you think otherwise you are wrong and your corn hole should be turned into a pocket for your unicorn's horn.

People also put forth the empty charade according to which life without god is meaningless.

Which is fucking stupid since you don't need to find the meaning of life… *outside of life*.

Postulating god as the source of our needs for meaning, values and morals does not certify his existence.

**That would be like saying that the gifts you received last Christmas prove the existence of Santa Claus.**

This would make you a fucking retarded *Homo sapiens*. And by homo, this time I mean butt stuffer.

Now get this: If god created me, then he created evil as well as good. That's not a perfect being by any standards. Also, if he did not create me, then he is a limited god and not an omnipotent entity.

Why doesn't he intervene in the suffering of the world?

Many people argue that men create their own suffering and not god; however, this is not true.

A lot of suffering in the world comes from disease or natural catastrophes, all sorts of things which are god's creations too.

This forces us to conclude that god is not all good and not all powerful.

As a matter of fact, he sounds more like He-Man's antagonist and arch-enemy Skeletor from Masters of the Universe, if you asked me.

**Humans are permanently in a tragic position:**

They are religious because they know they are going to die like their loved ones (or believe that they will get sucked up into the sky by some holy Hoover, if you're one of those Rapture-freaks).

This provides the religious wandering the driving force to maintain the convenient concept of faith which by the way is a concept very similar to the one of schizophrenia:

Believing in things that don't exist "yet," and pretending that they do.

**I say just take some mushrooms or acid and you can bypass the whole thing of going to church on Sunday.**

In the case of religion, faith is used the same way politicians use diplomatic immunity, they use the Bible like diplomats use the law: at their discretion.

So next time you find yourself in catechism or at a peace vigil do me a favor and kick someone's ass.

There is a good reason why jesus died wearing diapers.

Cheers,

-SATAN

www.ingramcontent.com/pod-product-compliance
Ingram Content Group UK Ltd.
Pitfield, Milton Keynes, MK11 3LW, UK
UKHW020129250726
13967UKWH00002B/550